THE ROLE OF SOCIAL MEDIA IN THE 2024 ELECTION

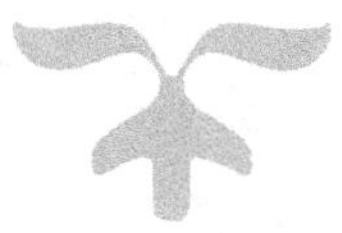

BY
KAREN RODMAN

To Zachary, my vote is for your future.

Table of Contents

Chapter 1

~~~~

The Rise of Social Media in Politics
~~~~

In recent years, social media has fundamentally changed the way politics operates. From how candidates engage with voters to the rapid dissemination of information and, unfortunately, misinformation, platforms like Twitter (now X), Facebook, and TikTok are now central to political campaigns. Social media's influence has transformed modern elections, allowing for direct communication between politicians and the public, reshaping the traditional media landscape, and giving rise to a new form of digital activism. This book explores the rise of social media in politics, its role in shaping elections, and the opportunities and challenges it presents to democracy.

The Beginnings: The Obama Campaign and Social Media's Breakthrough

While social media was used in smaller ways during earlier elections, it wasn't until Barack Obama's 2008 presidential campaign that it became a powerful political tool. Obama's campaign team used platforms like Facebook and YouTube to mobilize young voters, raise funds, and spread campaign messages. By integrating digital strategy into traditional campaign efforts, they were able to reach millions of voters at a lower cost compared to traditional media such as television and radio.

Obama's use of social media also marked a turning point in political fundraising. The campaign used digital tools to enable small donations from everyday supporters, revolutionizing how campaigns could finance their efforts. Rather than relying solely on wealthy donors and PACs, the campaign democratized fundraising and connected directly with supporters. The success of this strategy would set the stage for future elections.

—~—

The Trump Era: Twitter and the Dominance of Social Media in Politics

If Obama's 2008 campaign showcased social media's potential, Donald Trump's use of Twitter in the 2016 election cemented its role as a central element of modern political campaigns. Trump's unfiltered and frequent use of Twitter allowed him to bypass traditional media outlets, control his own narrative, and reach millions of followers directly. He made Twitter his megaphone, using it to attack opponents, spread campaign promises, and stoke controversy, all while garnering massive media coverage.

Trump's digital strategy was not limited to Twitter. His campaign utilized targeted Facebook ads, data analytics, and digital marketing to great effect. Facebook's powerful ad platform allowed the Trump campaign to tailor messages to specific demographic groups and swing voters, micro-targeting key areas in battleground states. In fact, some argue that social media's ability to deliver highly personalized messages played a pivotal role in Trump's surprise victory in 2016.

—~—

The Role of Social Media in Voter Engagement and Mobilization

Social media's rise has not only altered how candidates run their campaigns but also how voters engage with politics. Platforms like Twitter, Facebook, and TikTok enable real-time discussions, giving citizens the opportunity to interact directly with candidates, express opinions, and participate in political discourse. In many ways, social media has lowered the barrier for political participation, empowering more people to share their views and get involved.

Furthermore, social media has become a critical tool for mobilizing voters. Hashtags like **#BlackLivesMatter** or **#MeToo** have transcended individual causes, fueling movements that have shaped the political conversation. These digital movements can bring attention to important social justice issues and prompt politicians to address concerns that may otherwise be ignored by mainstream media.

During elections, social media also becomes a hub for grassroots organizing. Campaign volunteers and supporters use these platforms to coordinate events, organize door-knocking efforts, and encourage voter turnout. In the 2020 election, for example, many younger voters were mobilized through TikTok and Instagram campaigns that encouraged them to register to vote and head to the polls.

--~--

The Challenge of Misinformation and Echo Chambers

While social media has democratized political engagement, it has also introduced significant challenges, particularly the spread of misinformation and the rise of echo chambers. Misinformation, or false and misleading content, has become a pervasive issue on social media platforms. During the 2016 and 2020 U.S. elections, foreign actors and domestic groups alike spread fake news stories to influence voter perceptions and sow discord.

Social media algorithms, designed to keep users engaged by showing content they are likely to agree with, can also create echo chambers. In these digital spaces, users are only exposed to viewpoints that align with their own, reinforcing biases and making it more difficult for individuals to encounter differing perspectives. This polarization can have serious consequences for democracy, as it undermines informed decision-making and fosters division within society.

Major social media platforms have taken steps to combat misinformation, such as flagging false content, fact-checking posts, and banning accounts that spread harmful conspiracy theories. However, these efforts have faced criticism for either being too lenient or too aggressive, further highlighting the complexities of regulating speech in the digital age.

--~--

The Future of Social Media in Politics

As we look toward future elections, social media will continue to play an integral role in politics. The use of video-based platforms like TikTok is already shifting the landscape. Candidates and activists are using short-form videos to engage younger voters, spread political messages, and create viral moments that can impact public opinion.

However, the evolving nature of these platforms raises new questions. How will regulations adapt to the fast-paced, ever-changing world of social media? What role will artificial intelligence play in targeting voters? And how will we balance free speech with the need to prevent misinformation?

The rise of social media in politics has transformed how campaigns are run, how voters engage with issues, and how political messages are disseminated. While these platforms offer unprecedented opportunities for engagement and mobilization, they also present new challenges that must be addressed to ensure a healthy democratic process. As the 2024 election approaches, the role of social media will undoubtedly continue to shape the future of political campaigns and civic participation.

Chapter 2

~~~~

How Political Campaigns Leverage Social Media
~~~~

In today's digital age, social media has become one of the most powerful tools for political campaigns. It is no longer just a means to share updates or engage casually with voters—it has evolved into a sophisticated platform for advertising, voter outreach, data analytics, and even grassroots organizing. Platforms like Facebook, Twitter, Instagram, and TikTok offer campaigns unprecedented access to potential voters. By using targeted ads, real-time interaction, and viral content, campaigns can maximize their influence with minimal expenditure compared to traditional media. Political campaigns strategically leverage social media to shape public perception and engage voters.

Targeted Advertising and Microtargeting

One of the most significant advantages of social media is its ability to offer targeted advertising. Platforms like Facebook and Google allow political campaigns to reach specific voter demographics based on their behavior, interests, and online activity. For example, if someone frequently engages with content about climate change, a political campaign can deliver ads that highlight the candidate's stance on environmental policies directly to that user.

This ability to microtarget different segments of the population is a game-changer for political campaigns. Instead of delivering a one-size-fits-all message through television or radio, campaigns can tailor messages to different groups. A conservative candidate might target older voters with ads focused on traditional values and economic stability, while a progressive candidate could reach younger voters with content about student debt relief and climate action.

Microtargeting enables campaigns to create hundreds, even thousands, of versions of the same ad, slightly tweaking the message, tone, or imagery to suit specific audiences. During the 2016 U.S. election, for instance, the Trump campaign ran thousands of versions of ads aimed at different voters, testing which messages resonated most effectively in real time. The result was a highly efficient use of resources that maximized voter engagement and, some argue, influenced the outcome of the election.

--~--

Data Analytics: Leveraging Voter Data

Social media platforms collect vast amounts of data from users, which political campaigns can analyze to craft more effective strategies. Data analytics enables campaigns to understand voter behavior, identify key demographics, and track engagement levels. By studying likes, shares, retweets, and comments, campaigns can determine which issues voters care about most, where they stand politically, and how they are likely to vote.

During the 2012 U.S. presidential election, Barack Obama's campaign famously used data analytics to great effect. The campaign's data team collected and analyzed millions of data points to create voter profiles and determine the most effective outreach methods. Obama's team used predictive modeling to identify undecided voters and target them with personalized messages. This data-driven approach not only helped optimize advertising strategies but also ensured that the campaign's resources were directed toward the most critical voters.

In addition to direct data from platforms, campaigns can use third-party data to enhance their targeting. For example, data firms like Cambridge Analytica have harvested information from social media users to help craft hyper-specific voter outreach strategies. While the use of such data raises significant ethical concerns, it has undeniably proven effective in shaping campaign outcomes.

--~--

Real-Time Interaction and Rapid Response

Social media allows political campaigns to engage in real-time interaction with voters, making it one of the most dynamic tools available to modern politicians. Candidates can post updates, respond to questions, and address breaking news instantly. This direct connection with voters builds a sense of authenticity and accessibility that traditional media cannot match.

Platforms like Twitter are especially popular for real-time engagement. Politicians can comment on current events, rebut criticism, or make policy announcements on the fly. This rapid-response ability is crucial for maintaining control of the narrative during a campaign. For example, if a negative story surfaces about a candidate, their campaign can immediately issue a statement or clarification via social media, mitigating potential damage before it spirals out of control.

Additionally, live streaming on platforms like Facebook, Instagram, and TikTok has become a vital tool for campaigns. Candidates can hold virtual town halls, answer live questions from voters, and share behind-the-scenes moments. This format not only makes politicians seem more approachable but also allows them to reach a larger, geographically diverse audience.

--~--

The Power of Viral Content and Memes

One of the most unique and influential aspects of social media is the ability for content to go viral. Viral content—posts, videos, or memes that spread rapidly across the internet—can have a profound impact on public perception. Political campaigns capitalize on this by creating shareable, engaging content designed to resonate with specific audiences.

Memes have become a particularly effective tool in political communication, especially among younger voters. Short, humorous, and often satirical, memes condense complex political ideas into bite-sized content that can be easily shared. During the 2020 Democratic primaries, Bernie Sanders' campaign effectively used memes to engage with younger voters, creating viral content that portrayed Sanders as relatable and in tune with their concerns.

Social media platforms like TikTok, with its short video format, have become particularly effective for creating viral political content. Campaigns and supporters can produce engaging clips that highlight key issues, show support for candidates, or criticize opponents. These videos, often crafted with humor or emotion, can reach millions of people in just a few hours.

--~--

Grassroots Movements and Digital Activism

Social media has enabled the rise of grassroots movements that can organize, fundraise, and advocate for candidates in ways that were previously impossible. Movements like Black Lives Matter and #MeToo started on social media and gained momentum through widespread online engagement. These movements bring attention to issues that might be ignored by traditional media and can pressure political campaigns to address them.

Candidates themselves also rely on digital activism to build support. Platforms like GoFundMe or ActBlue allow campaigns to crowdfund directly from their supporters, cutting out the need for large donors or political action committees (PACs). Supporters can donate small amounts of money, organize events, and mobilize voters all through social media. This digital grassroots support has become critical for candidates who lack traditional political backing but can energize a base through online platforms.

--~--

The Future of Political Campaigns and Social Media

As political campaigns continue to evolve, social media will undoubtedly play an even more prominent role in shaping elections.

With the ability to target specific voter groups, analyze vast amounts of data, and engage with voters in real-time, platforms like Facebook, Twitter, and TikTok provide politicians with powerful tools to influence the electorate. However, the rise of misinformation, ethical concerns about data use, and the creation of echo chambers present new challenges that campaigns and platforms must address. Moving forward, political campaigns will need to balance the power of social media with transparency, ethics, and accountability to maintain public trust.

Chapter 3

~~~~

The Dark Side of Social Media: Misinformation and Fake News
~~~~

Social media has transformed the way we connect, share information, and engage with the world. It provides platforms for instant communication, the spread of ideas, and the mobilization of grassroots movements. However, this unprecedented connectivity has a darker side—misinformation and fake news. In recent years, social media platforms like Facebook, Twitter, and TikTok have become breeding grounds for false and misleading content, contributing to public confusion, division, and even political instability. The consequences of this trend are far-reaching, affecting elections, public health, and social cohesion.

What is Misinformation and Fake News?

Misinformation refers to false or inaccurate information that is spread, regardless of whether there is an intent to deceive. In contrast, fake news often refers to fabricated news stories that are deliberately crafted to mislead or provoke a specific reaction. These terms have gained prominence in recent years, particularly in the context of political events like elections and public health crises such as the COVID-19 pandemic.

While misinformation can include simple errors or misunderstandings, fake news is often designed with more malicious intent, playing on the emotions and biases of the audience. These false narratives are engineered to look credible, with misleading headlines, fabricated quotes, or doctored images that mimic the style of legitimate news outlets.

--~--

The Mechanisms of Misinformation Spread on Social Media

The architecture of social media platforms makes it easy for misinformation and fake news to thrive. There are several key factors that contribute to the spread of false information on these platforms:

Virality and Engagement

Social media platforms thrive on virality—the rapid spread of content through user engagement, such as likes, shares, and comments. Algorithms on platforms like Facebook and Twitter prioritize content that elicits strong reactions, whether positive or negative. Unfortunately, misinformation is more likely to go viral than factual information because it often plays on emotions like fear, anger, or excitement. A study published in *Science* found that false news stories spread more quickly and widely than true stories, especially those that evoked feelings of surprise or disgust.

Echo Chambers and Filter Bubbles

As noted in previous chapters, social media platforms are designed to show users content they are more likely to engage with, creating filter bubbles—online spaces where users are mostly exposed to information that aligns with their existing beliefs and biases. This can create echo chambers, where misinformation is continuously reinforced by like-minded users, making it harder for people to encounter opposing viewpoints or fact-based content.

For example, a person who frequently engages with conspiracy theories about climate change might see more content that denies climate science, further entrenching their views. This self-reinforcing cycle makes it difficult for credible information to break through the bubble of misinformation.

The Role of Bots and Trolls

The spread of misinformation is often accelerated by bots—automated accounts that can post, like, or share content on social media. Bots can amplify misinformation by making it appear more popular and widely accepted than it actually is. Similarly, trolls—individuals or groups who deliberately post inflammatory or false content—use social media to spread disinformation and provoke emotional responses.

During the 2016 U.S. presidential election, for instance, Russian troll farms and bot networks were found to have played a significant role in spreading divisive and false information on social media platforms to influence public opinion and sow discord.

--~--

The Impact of Misinformation on Society

The consequences of misinformation and fake news extend far beyond individual social media posts. The spread of false information can have profound and lasting effects on society, from influencing political outcomes to eroding trust in public institutions.

Undermining Democracy

Misinformation has the potential to undermine the democratic process by distorting the information that voters use to make informed decisions. During elections, false news stories can be used to manipulate public opinion, attack political opponents, or discredit electoral systems. For example, during the 2020 U.S. election, widespread false claims about voter fraud were circulated on social media, leading to confusion, mistrust, and in some cases, violence.

When people are exposed to a barrage of false or misleading information, it can create *disinformation fatigue*, where they become skeptical of all news sources, even credible ones. This erodes public trust in the media, government, and the democratic process itself, as people struggle to distinguish between fact and fiction.

Public Health Risks

The COVID-19 pandemic highlighted the dangers of health-related misinformation on social media. False claims about the virus, such as rumors that it was a hoax or that certain unproven remedies could cure it, spread widely across platforms like Facebook, YouTube, and WhatsApp. In some cases, misinformation led people to avoid wearing masks, refuse vaccinations, or seek dangerous treatments, contributing to preventable deaths and prolonging the pandemic.

Public health experts have struggled to counteract this "infodemic" of misinformation, which often moves faster than scientific findings or official statements from health authorities.

Social Polarization and Division

Misinformation, particularly when politically motivated, can deepen societal divisions by reinforcing existing biases and stoking anger. Social media platforms, by prioritizing emotionally charged content, contribute to a cycle of polarization in which people become more entrenched in their views and less open to compromise or dialogue. This division can lead to heightened conflict between different political, social, or ethnic groups, as misinformation fosters misunderstanding and mistrust.

--~--

Combating Misinformation and Fake News

Addressing the spread of misinformation requires a multifaceted approach that involves both individual responsibility and systemic changes to the way social media platforms operate.

Media Literacy

One of the most effective ways to combat misinformation is through media literacy—educating people on how to critically evaluate the information they encounter online. Schools and organizations can play a role in teaching individuals to verify sources, cross-check facts, and recognize biased or misleading content. Simple techniques, such as searching for the original source of a claim or checking multiple news outlets, can go a long way in preventing the spread of misinformation.

Fact-Checking and Reporting Misinformation

Fact-checking organizations, such as Snopes, FactCheck.org, and Politifact, play a critical role in debunking false claims. Social media platforms have also introduced fact-checking features that flag or remove content deemed misleading. Users themselves can report suspicious posts, helping platforms identify and take down harmful content before it spreads further.

Platform Accountability

Social media companies have faced increasing pressure to take responsibility for the content shared on their platforms. Some have implemented changes, such as tweaking their algorithms to reduce the spread of false information, removing bots, or banning accounts that repeatedly violate community guidelines. However, critics argue that these measures often don't go far enough and that more robust regulations and oversight are needed.

Governments worldwide are considering legislation to hold platforms accountable for the spread of misinformation, though these efforts are complicated by concerns over censorship and free speech.

--~--

The Ongoing Battle Against Misinformation

Misinformation and fake news represent a growing challenge in the digital age. As social media continues to shape public discourse, it is essential for individuals, platforms, and governments to work together to mitigate the spread of false information. While progress has been made in raising awareness and introducing fact-checking measures, the fight against misinformation is far from over. In a world where misinformation can spread faster than ever before, maintaining an informed and vigilant public is critical to preserving the integrity of democratic institutions and the health of our societies.

Chapter 4

~~~~

How to Avoid Misinformation in 2024
~~~~

As the world becomes more connected through the internet and social media, the challenge of navigating false information—also known as misinformation—continues to grow. With the 2024 elections approaching, the spread of misinformation is likely to increase, making it more critical than ever to be vigilant about the information we consume and share. From conspiracy theories to manipulated images and sensational headlines, misinformation can easily sway public opinion, skew perceptions, and negatively influence decision-making. The following provides practical tips on how to avoid misinformation, including how to fact-check, question information before sharing it on social media, and verify information from multiple sources.

Understand What Misinformation Is

As we discussed previously, misinformation is false or misleading information that is spread, regardless of whether there is an intent to deceive. It can range from innocent misunderstandings to deliberate disinformation campaigns designed to manipulate opinions or undermine trust in institutions. The 2024 election is likely to see a wave of misinformation due to the increasing use of social media, the polarization of political opinions, and the high stakes involved.

To avoid falling prey to misinformation, it's important to first understand that not everything we see online is credible. Fake news, misleading articles, or out-of-context claims are often engineered to look legitimate but may lack factual basis. The more emotional the content makes you feel, the more you should question its validity—fake news thrives on stirring strong emotions, such as fear or anger, which leads to higher engagement.

Fact-Check Before Believing or Sharing

One of the most effective ways to combat misinformation is to use fact-checking resources before believing or sharing information. Numerous independent fact-checking organizations, such as Snopes, FactCheck.org, and *Politifact*, are dedicated to verifying claims made by politicians, media outlets, and social media users. These websites often have entire sections devoted to debunking popular myths, viral content, and misinformation.

When encountering a claim online, take a moment to visit one of these sites and search for information related to the topic. For example, if you see a sensational story about an election conspiracy, enter the headline or keywords into these fact-checking websites to see if they have investigated the claim. Often, you'll find well-researched articles that either confirm or debunk the information.

Tip: Bookmark fact-checking sites in your browser for quick access when you encounter questionable content.

--~--

Question the Source Before Sharing

Before you share any information on social media or in conversations with friends, it's essential to question the source. Ask yourself the following:

- ? Who published this information? Is it from a reputable news organization, a government website, or an established nonprofit? Or is it from an unknown source, blog, or website with a questionable reputation?
- ? What is the purpose of this content? Is it meant to inform, persuade, entertain, or provoke an emotional reaction? Misinformation often plays on emotions like fear, outrage, or anger to get people to share it without thinking critically.
- ? Are there red flags? Watch out for poor grammar, sensationalist headlines, and lack of citations or credible sources. These can be indicators that the content is unreliable or misleading.

Social media thrives on instant reactions and engagement, but pausing before sharing can help prevent the spread of misinformation. The act of sharing false information—even unknowingly—helps it reach a wider audience, which can have real-world consequences, such as spreading panic or reinforcing false narratives.

--~--

Check Multiple Sources

A key tip for avoiding misinformation is to check multiple sources before accepting a piece of information as true. If you see a news article or social media post that makes an unusual or extraordinary claim, verify it by finding other trustworthy news outlets or websites that report on the same issue.

For instance, if a claim is circulating about a major political scandal, reputable media organizations such as The New York Times, BBC, or The Associated Press will cover it if it is legitimate. If only fringe websites or partisan blogs are reporting on the claim, that should raise a red flag.

Tip: Try to diversify your news consumption by following a variety of outlets, including those with differing political perspectives. This helps prevent falling into an echo chamber, where you only see information that reinforces your existing views.

--~--

Be Wary of Sensationalist Content and Clickbait

Clickbait refers to content that uses exaggerated or misleading headlines to attract attention and generate clicks. Often, clickbait articles contain sensationalist information that plays on emotions but lacks credible evidence or context. Headlines like "You Won't Believe What This Politician Did!" or "The Shocking Truth About [Issue]" are designed to provoke curiosity and engagement but often lack substance.

If a headline sounds too outrageous or extreme to be true, it's wise to be skeptical. Click on the article to read beyond the headline—sometimes, the body of the article will provide context that deflates the sensationalism of the headline. If the article doesn't back up its claims with credible sources, dismiss it as unreliable.

Tip: Avoid sharing articles based solely on headlines. Many people share articles on social media without reading them first, which contributes to the spread of misinformation.

--~--

Examine Images and Videos Carefully

Misinformation isn't limited to text-based content. In fact, images and videos can be manipulated or taken out of context to create misleading narratives. For example, a photograph from a past event may be circulated as evidence of a current situation, or a video may be edited to omit important context, changing its meaning entirely.

To verify the authenticity of images and videos, you can use tools like Google Reverse Image Search. This tool allows you to upload an image or paste the image URL to find where it originally appeared and determine whether it has been misused. Similarly, websites like InVID offer tools to verify videos by breaking them into keyframes and checking them against reliable sources.

--~--

Question Viral Content

Content that spreads quickly, especially on platforms like TikTok and Twitter, can often be misleading. Viral content thrives on emotional engagement, and people may share it without checking its accuracy. Before believing viral stories, ask yourself:

? Why is this going viral? Is it because it is sensational, shocking, or playing into current fears?

? Who is sharing this? If it's being shared by anonymous accounts, fringe groups, or bots, it may not be reliable.

? Viral content is often created for the purpose of generating attention rather than providing accurate information. Remember, the faster a story spreads, the more likely it is to be incomplete or misleading.

--~--

Engage in Discussions, but Be Skeptical

While social media provides opportunities to engage in political and social discussions, it's essential to approach these conversations with skepticism. People often post opinions or biased interpretations of events rather than factual reporting. Be open to engaging in dialogue, but always verify claims with credible sources before forming strong opinions or arguments.

If someone shares a claim that seems questionable, politely ask for a source or provide a verified link that offers a clearer perspective. While not everyone is open to changing their views, sharing reliable information can help create a healthier dialogue.

--~--

Stay Informed, Stay Skeptical

In 2024, with an important election looming, the stakes are high, and misinformation will continue to be a significant issue. By fact-checking information, questioning before sharing, and checking multiple sources, you can protect yourself from falling prey to misinformation. Engaging with social media critically and thoughtfully will ensure that you remain informed and make decisions based on reliable information, not falsehoods or exaggerations. The key to navigating the digital age is skepticism, vigilance, and a commitment to the truth.

25

Chapter 5

~~~~

Social Media and Election Influence
~~~~

In the modern political landscape, social media has become an essential platform for engaging voters, spreading information, and influencing electoral outcomes. With billions of users worldwide, platforms like Facebook, Twitter, Instagram, and TikTok have revolutionized how political campaigns communicate with the public. However, these platforms also provide fertile ground for the rapid spread of misinformation and polarization. Let's break down how social media influences voter behavior, examine case studies from the 2016 and 2020 U.S. presidential elections, and discuss the power of memes in shaping public opinion.

Social Media's Impact on Voter Behavior

Social media has a significant influence on how voters perceive candidates, issues, and political narratives. Unlike traditional media, social media platforms provide users with personalized content based on algorithms that track their behavior, preferences, and interactions. This can lead to the creation of echo chambers—digital spaces where individuals are exposed only to information that aligns with their existing beliefs.

Personalization and Microtargeting

One of the most profound ways social media affects voter behavior is through personalized advertising and microtargeting. Political campaigns use detailed data about voters' interests, demographics, and behaviors to deliver tailored messages that resonate with specific audiences. For example, in the 2016 U.S. presidential election, Donald Trump's campaign utilized Facebook's advanced targeting tools to deliver thousands of different ads to voters, each tailored to specific interests, concerns, or regions.

Microtargeting allows campaigns to craft highly specific messages, from economic concerns in the Rust Belt to immigration issues in border states, ensuring that voters see content that appeals directly to them. While this can be an effective way to engage voters, it also raises concerns about the potential for manipulation, as campaigns may present information in a way that distorts the full picture of an issue or candidate.

Echo Chambers and Confirmation Bias

Social media platforms, driven by algorithms, often amplify content that users are likely to engage with, creating echo chambers where people are primarily exposed to information that reinforces their pre-existing views. This phenomenon can lead to *confirmation bias*, where individuals accept information that aligns with their beliefs without critically evaluating its validity.

In political contexts, echo chambers can polarize voters by deepening ideological divisions. For example, a user who frequently engages with conservative content may see more politically conservative articles, memes, and ads, while liberal voters experience the opposite. As a result, voters may become more entrenched in their positions, less willing to engage with opposing viewpoints, and more susceptible to misinformation.

--~--

Case Study: The 2016 U.S. Presidential Election

The 2016 U.S. presidential election was a turning point in understanding the role social media plays in influencing elections. Donald Trump's use of Twitter, Facebook, and other platforms became a central feature of his campaign, while Hillary Clinton's campaign focused more on traditional media strategies. Trump's unconventional and often controversial posts on Twitter allowed him to dominate the news cycle and maintain direct engagement with his supporters.

Facebook and Data Analytics

One of the most discussed aspects of the 2016 election was the role of Facebook and the use of voter data by political consulting firms like Cambridge Analytica. The firm harvested data from millions of Facebook users without their consent, using this information to create psychological profiles of voters. These profiles allowed the Trump campaign to microtarget voters with specific ads designed to trigger emotional responses and influence their decisions at the polls.

According to reports, Cambridge Analytica delivered targeted ads to undecided voters, particularly in swing states, with the goal of either persuading them to vote for Trump or discouraging them from voting for Clinton. This use of microtargeting and psychological manipulation raised ethical concerns about the extent to which social media data could be used to influence elections.

Misinformation and Russian Interference

Another critical factor in the 2016 election was the spread of misinformation on social media, much of which was attributed to Russian interference. Investigations revealed that Russian operatives, posing as U.S. citizens, created fake accounts and pages on platforms like Facebook and Twitter to spread divisive content and misinformation aimed at influencing voters.

These operatives targeted key demographic groups, such as African Americans, with fake news stories designed to suppress voter turnout for Hillary Clinton. The content often included fabricated stories, memes, and misleading headlines that were widely shared and engaged with, amplifying their reach and impact on voters.

Case Study: The 2020 U.S. Presidential Election

The 2020 U.S. presidential election, held amid a global pandemic, saw an even greater reliance on social media platforms as candidates adapted to the realities of reduced in-person campaigning. Social media became the primary battlefield for shaping public opinion and engaging voters in real-time.

Joe Biden's Digital Strategy

Joe Biden's campaign utilized a digital-first strategy, leveraging platforms like Instagram, TikTok, and Facebook to reach younger voters and minority communities. His team focused on promoting key policy initiatives, such as COVID-19 recovery plans and healthcare reforms, while also countering misinformation spread by opponents.

One of the standout aspects of Biden's social media strategy was his focus on authenticity and relatability. His campaign frequently posted behind-the-scenes videos, live streams, and personal stories, which helped humanize the candidate and build trust with voters.

The Role of Misinformation and Fact-Checking

Misinformation continued to play a significant role in the 2020 election, with false claims about voter fraud, mail-in ballots, and COVID-19 circulating widely on social media. However, platforms like Twitter and Facebook introduced fact-checking features and labels to flag misleading content. Twitter, for instance, frequently flagged or removed tweets from both candidates that contained false or misleading claims about the election.

Despite these efforts, misinformation still reached millions of users, underscoring the ongoing challenge of combating false information on social media platforms.

The Power of Memes in Shaping Public Opinion

In recent years, memes have emerged as a powerful tool for influencing political opinions, particularly among younger voters. Memes are easily shareable, often humorous images or videos with brief text that convey a message quickly. In the context of elections, memes can simplify complex political ideas into bite-sized, relatable content that spreads rapidly across social media platforms.

Memes in the 2016 Election

During the 2016 U.S. election, memes played a significant role in shaping public perceptions of the candidates. Pro-Trump communities on platforms like Reddit and 4chan created memes that ridiculed Hillary Clinton and highlighted Trump's populist rhetoric. The Pepe the Frog meme, for example, became a symbol of the alt-right movement and was frequently used in political discourse.

Memes allowed Trump's supporters to connect with each other, build a sense of community, and create a counter-narrative to traditional media outlets. Memes also contributed to Trump's anti-establishment persona, positioning him as a political outsider who could disrupt the status quo.

Memes in the 2020 Election

In the 2020 election, memes once again played a significant role in shaping public discourse. Pro-Biden memes circulated widely on Instagram and TikTok, particularly among younger voters who used humor to engage with political content. Memes that highlighted Biden's policies or poked fun at Trump's handling of the COVID-19 pandemic went viral, helping to energize voter turnout among millennials and Gen Z.

The viral nature of memes makes them an effective tool for campaigns to reach wide audiences, particularly those who might not engage with traditional political messaging. However, memes can also spread misinformation if they simplify issues too much or distort facts.

--~--

Social Media's Evolving Role in Elections

Social media has fundamentally changed how elections are fought and won. Its ability to influence voter behavior, spread information quickly, and mobilize grassroots movements makes it a powerful tool for political campaigns. However, the same features that make social media effective—virality, personalization, and engagement—also make it a breeding ground for misinformation, polarization, and manipulation.

As the 2024 election approaches, the role of social media will continue to evolve, with platforms likely introducing more fact-checking measures and voters becoming more aware of the need for critical evaluation of online content. Nonetheless, the power of social media to shape public opinion and influence electoral outcomes remains undeniable, highlighting both its potential and its risks for democracy.

Chapter 6

~~~~

Making Smart Choices in the Social Media Era
~~~~

In the digital age, social media has become an integral part of our daily lives, shaping how we consume information, engage with others, and form our opinions on important issues. Platforms like Twitter, Facebook, Instagram, and TikTok offer unprecedented access to a wide range of voices and viewpoints, allowing people to engage with news, politics, and social issues in real time. However, the constant flow of information and the rise of echo chambers make it increasingly difficult to discern fact from fiction and avoid polarization. Let's explore how to make smart choices in the social media era, focusing on listening to a variety of voices, staying engaged in discussions while avoiding extreme views, and developing a deeper understanding of the issues.

The Importance of Listening to a Variety of Voices

One of the greatest advantages of social media is the ability to connect with people from all walks of life, giving us access to a diverse range of opinions and experiences. However, many people fall into the trap of following only like-minded individuals or news sources that reinforce their existing beliefs. These echo chambers, where users are exposed solely to information that aligns with their worldview, limit their ability to consider other perspectives.

Listening to a variety of voices—both those you agree with and those you don't—helps broaden your understanding of complex issues. When you expose yourself to different viewpoints, you're more likely to develop a well-rounded perspective and become more empathetic toward others. This doesn't mean that you have to agree with everything you read or hear, but being open to different ideas fosters critical thinking and challenges you to reflect on your own beliefs.

For example, instead of relying solely on one news outlet or social media account, follow a mix of voices, including those from different political affiliations, countries, and social backgrounds. You could follow a conservative commentator alongside a liberal journalist, or a climate activist alongside a business leader. This approach encourages a more comprehensive view of the issues and allows you to see how different communities interpret the same events.

--~--

Staying Engaged in Discussions While Avoiding Extreme Views

Engaging in discussions on social media is an important way to participate in democratic dialogue, share ideas, and learn from others. However, it's crucial to approach these discussions with care. Social media often amplifies extreme voices—those who hold radical or polarizing views—because sensational content tends to generate more engagement. While it may be tempting to dive into debates with these extreme voices, doing so can be counterproductive and may lead to frustration or increased polarization.

To make smart choices, focus on constructive discussions with people who are willing to engage in good-faith dialogue. Look for conversations that are solution-oriented rather than conflict-driven. Avoid getting sucked into arguments with people who are more interested in shouting their opinions than in listening or finding common ground. Instead, seek out individuals who are respectful, curious, and open to understanding different viewpoints.

That being said, it's important not to dismiss someone's argument simply because it seems extreme to you. Sometimes, individuals with unconventional views can offer insights that challenge the status quo or provide valuable criticism. However, it's crucial to assess whether the person is open to dialogue or simply pushing an agenda. If someone is unwilling to consider other perspectives or engages in inflammatory language, it's often best to disengage and focus on more meaningful conversations.

--~--

Understanding the Issues: Doing Your Own Research

In the age of social media, it's easy to feel like an expert on any given topic simply by scrolling through your news feed. However, headlines, memes, and tweets rarely provide the depth needed to fully understand complex social and political issues. To make informed decisions, especially when it comes to voting or advocating for change, it's essential to go beyond social media snippets and do your own research.

Understanding the issues requires looking at multiple sources and diving deeper into the topics that matter to you. When you come across a controversial claim or a sensational headline, resist the urge to take it at face value. Instead, ask yourself:

? Where is this information coming from? Is it from a reputable news organization, a government agency, or an expert in the field?

? Is there bias in the presentation? Every source has some degree of bias, but understanding who is delivering the message can help you determine the credibility of the information.

? What do other sources say about this issue? Don't rely on a single article or post. Look for other sources that offer different angles or corroborate the information.

For example, during the 2020 U.S. presidential election, many false claims circulated about mail-in voting and voter fraud. Fact-checking organizations like FactCheck.org, Snopes, and *Politifact* provided in-depth explanations debunking many of these myths. By seeking out credible sources and comparing information across multiple outlets, you can develop a clearer and more accurate understanding of the issues at hand.

It's also valuable to engage with long-form content—such as books, documentaries, or expert interviews—that provide more in-depth analysis than the rapid-fire content of social media. Long-form content allows you to explore topics in greater detail and helps you avoid the superficiality of viral content.

Avoiding Misinformation and Disinformation

In the social media era, misinformation (unintentionally false information) and disinformation (deliberately misleading information) are rampant. They can distort public opinion, incite fear, and damage trust in public institutions. To make smart choices in the face of misinformation, follow these practical tips:

- Fact-check before sharing: Before you share a post, article, or meme, verify its accuracy using fact-checking websites like Snopes, FactCheck.org, and Politifact. If something seems too good (or bad) to be true, it probably is.
- Question sensational content: Misinformation often spreads because it plays on strong emotions like fear, anger, or joy. Be skeptical of posts that seem designed to provoke an emotional reaction, especially if they lack credible sources.
- Recognize bots and trolls: Some social media accounts are not real people but are designed to spread disinformation and sow discord. If an account seems suspicious, posts inflammatory content without context, or engages in trolling behavior, it's likely a bot or troll. Reporting these accounts helps curb the spread of disinformation.

By taking the time to assess the information you encounter and question its credibility, you can avoid contributing to the spread of misinformation and ensure that the information you rely on is accurate and trustworthy.

--~--

Navigating the Social Media Landscape

Social media offers incredible opportunities for connection, learning, and engagement, but it also presents challenges, particularly in distinguishing credible information from misinformation. By listening to a variety of voices, staying engaged in respectful discussions, and doing your own research to understand the issues, you can make smart choices in the social media era. It's important to remain open-minded but skeptical, aware but thoughtful, and engaged but critical. Ultimately, making informed choices on social media is about cultivating a balanced, nuanced perspective that helps you navigate the flood of information in today's digital world.

Chapter 7

~~~

Social Media as a Tool for Change
~~~

Social media has revolutionized the way individuals, communities, and even governments engage with the world. Once primarily a space for sharing personal updates and photos, platforms like Twitter, Facebook, Instagram, and TikTok have evolved into powerful tools for political activism, civic engagement, and social change. We will now explore how social media has become a crucial instrument for grassroots movements, the rise of crowdfunding and petitions, the rise of citizen journalism, and the way it bridges the gap between citizens and politicians by allowing direct engagement.

The Power of Grassroots Movements

Grassroots movements have long been a means for ordinary people to create social change, but the rise of social media has amplified their reach and influence in unprecedented ways. Before the digital age, organizing protests, petitions, or movements required significant resources and logistical efforts, limiting the scale and speed of such actions. Today, social media provides a platform where these movements can gain momentum quickly, sometimes going viral within hours.

The Role of Hashtags in Activism

Hashtags, simple phrases preceded by the "#" symbol, have become iconic tools for rallying people around a cause on social media. One of the most powerful examples of this is the #BlackLivesMatter movement, which originated in 2013 after the acquittal of George Zimmerman in the shooting death of Trayvon Martin. The hashtag has since become a global symbol of the fight against systemic racism and police brutality. Through the use of #BlackLivesMatter, activists were able to bring attention to the deaths of unarmed Black people, mobilize protests, and demand police reform.

Similarly, #MeToo, which gained widespread attention in 2017, highlighted the pervasive issue of sexual harassment and assault, especially in the workplace. What started as an online movement rapidly transformed into real-world actions, such as corporate policy changes, public discussions about gender inequality, and high-profile resignations of individuals accused of harassment.

The key to these movements' success lies in their ability to mobilize people globally, regardless of their physical location. Social media connects individuals from diverse backgrounds and allows them to contribute to the cause, whether through raising awareness, organizing protests, or donating to related organizations.

The Rise of Crowdfunding and Petitions

Social media has also facilitated the rise of crowdfunding and online petitions, making it easier for individuals to support causes they care about, even if they lack significant financial or political resources.

Crowdfunding for Social Change

Crowdfunding platforms like GoFundMe, Kickstarter, and Patreon allow people to raise money for social causes, from medical expenses to community projects, with the help of their social media networks. These platforms are increasingly being used to fund activist causes, such as legal defense funds, environmental projects, or grassroots political campaigns. A powerful example of this is the funding of protest bail funds during the 2020 George Floyd protests, where activists raised millions of dollars to support protesters arrested during demonstrations.

Crowdfunding allows individuals to take immediate action in supporting causes they believe in, often bypassing traditional financial institutions or large non-governmental organizations (NGOs). Moreover, with the power of viral sharing, campaigns can quickly attract donations from around the world, even for local or small-scale initiatives.

Petitions and Social Media Advocacy

Another tool that has gained momentum with the rise of social media is the online petition. Websites like Change.org and Avaaz enable people to create and sign petitions addressing a wide range of issues, from environmental protection to human rights. These petitions often go viral on social media platforms, amplifying their reach and increasing their chances of receiving attention from policymakers or media outlets.

For example, in 2019, a petition demanding justice for Breonna Taylor, a Black woman killed by police in her home, gathered millions of signatures. Social media users shared the petition widely, pressuring local and state governments to re-examine the case and demand accountability. Although petitions may not always lead to immediate policy change, they often serve as a powerful tool for raising awareness and signaling widespread public support for a cause.

The Role of Citizen Journalism

In the age of social media, everyone with a smartphone and internet connection can become a citizen journalist. This democratization of media allows individuals to report on issues and events in real-time, often bypassing traditional media outlets. Citizen journalism can bring attention to issues that mainstream media may overlook or cover only superficially.

Documenting Social Injustice

Citizen journalism played a pivotal role during the 2020 protests following the killing of George Floyd. Bystanders recorded the event on their phones and shared it on social media, sparking outrage and protests across the globe. Without citizen journalism, Floyd's death might not have received the global attention it did. Videos of the incident circulated across platforms like Twitter, Facebook, and Instagram, with millions of people bearing witness to the brutality that ignited one of the largest social justice movements in modern history.

This real-time reporting by citizens allows for greater transparency and accountability, particularly in situations where mainstream media coverage is limited or biased. Citizen journalism also empowers marginalized voices, allowing them to tell their stories without needing approval from traditional gatekeepers.

Challenges and Responsibilities

While citizen journalism has transformed the way we receive information, it also poses challenges. Misinformation and bias can easily spread when individuals report on events without the checks and balances typically applied in traditional journalism. As a result, it's important for users to critically evaluate the sources of information they consume on social media and cross-reference facts with credible news organizations.

--~--

Bridging the Gap Between Citizens and Politicians

One of the most transformative aspects of social media is its ability to bridge the gap between the public and their political representatives. In the past, politicians were often seen as distant figures, accessible only through speeches, interviews, or town halls. Today, social media allows for direct engagement between citizens and politicians, fostering a more immediate and personal form of interaction.

Engaging with Politicians Directly

Social media platforms like Twitter have become primary spaces where politicians communicate with their constituents. Voters can directly ask questions, raise concerns, or voice support for policies, and in many cases, politicians will respond in real time. This form of engagement gives citizens a sense of direct access to their elected officials, enhancing democratic participation.

For instance, U.S. Representative Alexandria Ocasio-Cortez (AOC) is known for her active presence on social media, where she regularly interacts with constituents and discusses political issues on platforms like Twitter and Instagram. AOC's live streams and posts not only provide insight into her legislative work but also offer an informal space for educating the public on complex political topics.

Holding Politicians Accountable

In addition to facilitating dialogue, social media also provides a platform for holding politicians accountable. Viral posts and hashtags can quickly expose corruption, hypocrisy, or dishonesty, pushing politicians to address issues they might otherwise ignore. The public can organize campaigns calling for politicians to be held responsible for their actions, from viral hashtags like #ResignNow to organized online protests.

--~--

The Power of Social Media for Change

Social media has revolutionized how individuals engage with social, political, and environmental issues. Through grassroots movements, crowdfunding, petitions, and citizen journalism, ordinary people have found new ways to advocate for change and amplify their voices. Furthermore, social media's ability to connect citizens directly with politicians offers a unique opportunity for more transparent and participatory governance. While challenges such as misinformation and online polarization persist, the potential for positive social change through social media is undeniable. As we continue to adapt to this digital landscape, the key will be using these platforms responsibly to foster a more just, informed, and connected world.

Chapter 8

~~~~

Think About Your Future When Choosing a Candidate
~~~~

In every election, voters are faced with the critical decision of choosing leaders who will shape the future of their community, state, or country. While it's easy to get caught up in media coverage, social media trends, or campaign buzzwords, making an informed decision requires looking beyond the hype and considering the long-term impacts of a candidate's policies. You must learn how to think about your future when choosing a candidate, focusing on the importance of looking past media narratives, evaluating long-term vs. short-term benefits, and understanding the power of your vote.

Look Beyond the Media Hype

Media plays a crucial role in providing information about political candidates, but it also shapes narratives that may emphasize spectacle over substance. Whether it's televised debates, soundbites, or viral moments on social media, the way candidates are portrayed can sometimes distract from the more critical questions about their policies, qualifications, and long-term vision. When choosing a candidate, it's essential to look beyond the media hype and dig deeper into their stances on important issues.

Social Media and the "Highlight Reel" Effect

Social media platforms like Twitter, TikTok, and Instagram have transformed how political campaigns communicate with voters. While these platforms provide direct access to candidates and enable real-time interaction, they often prioritize quick, attention-grabbing content over substantive policy discussions. Campaigns craft posts and videos designed to go viral, focusing on humor, emotion, or controversial statements to boost engagement.

While these posts may be entertaining or resonate on a personal level, it's important to recognize that they represent only a small piece of a much larger picture. Instead of relying solely on social media posts, make an effort to explore the policy details available on candidates' official websites or in long-form interviews. Many candidates post comprehensive policy plans outlining their approach to healthcare, climate change, education, and more. These documents can provide a clearer sense of what a candidate actually stands for, beyond the catchy slogans.

The Role of Traditional Media

Traditional media—television, newspapers, and radio—also has a significant influence on voters' perceptions of candidates. While it plays a vital role in reporting news, it's important to recognize that media outlets may have their own biases, whether political or corporate. Some media outlets may give more favorable coverage to certain candidates or amplify negative stories about others, creating a skewed picture of the election.

To make a more informed decision, it's helpful to consume media from multiple sources. By following news from a variety of outlets with different political perspectives, you can gain a more balanced understanding of the issues and avoid being swayed by any one narrative.

--~--

Consider the Long-Term Impacts, Not Just Short-Term Gains

One of the most critical aspects of choosing a candidate is thinking beyond short-term campaign promises and considering the long-term implications of their policies. While some candidates may propose quick fixes or promises that seem immediately appealing, it's important to assess how those policies will play out over time.

Short-Term vs. Long-Term Policies

During election campaigns, candidates often emphasize policies designed to deliver immediate benefits. For example, a promise to cut taxes might sound appealing to many voters, especially those who are struggling financially. However, it's important to ask how these tax cuts will be funded and what impact they will have on long-term issues like healthcare, education, or infrastructure.

In contrast, other candidates may advocate for policies that require significant investment upfront but promise long-term benefits. For example, expanding access to healthcare, investing in renewable energy, or improving public education may not yield immediate results, but these policies can strengthen the economy, improve public health, and enhance quality of life over the coming decades.

When evaluating a candidate, ask yourself:

- What are the long-term consequences of their policies?
- How will this candidate's decisions affect future generations?
- Are they addressing root causes of issues, or are they offering band-aid solutions?

Case Study: Climate Change

A clear example of long-term thinking vs. short-term gains is climate change policy. Some candidates may propose immediate economic relief by deregulating industries or expanding fossil fuel production. While these policies may result in short-term job creation or economic boosts, they could contribute to the worsening of climate-related problems in the future, such as extreme weather, food shortages, and rising sea levels.

On the other hand, candidates who support investment in green energy or carbon reduction may face criticism for the costs associated with such initiatives, but their long-term vision could lead to a more sustainable economy, healthier environment, and stronger global leadership in addressing climate change. Choosing a candidate who has a long-term plan for addressing environmental, economic, and social challenges is essential for securing a stable future.

--~--

Understand That Every Vote Matters

A common misconception in elections is that an individual vote doesn't make a difference, particularly in larger elections such as presidential races. However, every vote counts, and in many elections, the margins of victory can be razor-thin. By voting, you are not only exercising your democratic right but also shaping the future of your community, your country, and even the world.

The Impact of Your Vote

Elections can be decided by very slim margins, especially in local or regional races. Even in national elections, pivotal swing states or districts can be won or lost by just a few hundred or thousand votes. If enough people feel that their vote doesn't matter and choose not to participate, they may unknowingly help a candidate they oppose secure victory.

Moreover, your vote impacts more than just the candidates on the ballot. By electing representatives who align with your values, you influence how legislation is passed and how policies are implemented. Whether it's healthcare reform, criminal justice policies, or climate change initiatives, the candidates you vote for will shape the laws that affect your everyday life.

Civic Responsibility

Beyond the immediate results of an election, voting is also about civic responsibility. In a democracy, participation is key to ensuring that the government reflects the will of the people. When citizens choose not to vote, they surrender their voice and allow others to make decisions on their behalf. Regardless of your political views, voting is a way to engage with the democratic process and make sure that your voice is heard.

Voting for the Future

While short-term gains are often tempting, the decisions we make today will shape the future for ourselves and for future generations. When choosing a candidate, it's important to think about the type of world you want to live in 10, 20, or even 50 years from now. Will the policies proposed today promote sustainability, equity, and economic stability in the long run?

--~--

Choosing Wisely for the Future

Choosing a candidate is not just about agreeing with their rhetoric or liking their personality. It's about evaluating their policies, looking past media hype, and thinking critically about the long-term consequences of their decisions. By considering how a candidate's policies will impact future generations, avoiding the distractions of social media and sensationalism, and recognizing the importance of your vote, you can make informed choices that contribute to a better future for yourself and society as a whole.

Every election represents an opportunity to shape the future. When you go to the polls, think beyond today's headlines and consider the broader implications of your choice.

Chapter 9

~~~

Moving Forward: The Future of Social Media in Elections
~~~

Social media has transformed how political campaigns are run, how voters engage with candidates, and how elections are won. As platforms like Facebook, Twitter, Instagram, and TikTok continue to evolve, so too does their influence on political processes. As we look toward the 2028 election and beyond, the role of social media is expected to grow even more significant, reshaping not only campaign strategies but also how elections are regulated. This essay will explore what to expect in the future of social media and elections, focusing on evolving platforms like TikTok, the impact of changing regulations, and critical factors that will influence the relationship between social media and politics in the coming years.

What to Expect in 2028: The Increasing Role of Social Media

As we look ahead to the 2028 election, social media platforms will continue to play a pivotal role in shaping electoral outcomes. While platforms like Facebook and Twitter were dominant in past elections, newer platforms like TikTok are rising in importance, especially among younger voters.

The Rise of TikTok in Political Campaigns

TikTok, the short-form video platform, has gained immense popularity, particularly among Gen Z and millennial users. With over 1 billion active users worldwide, TikTok's potential to influence elections is profound. What sets TikTok apart from traditional platforms is its algorithm, which emphasizes virality and engagement over follower count. This means that political messages on TikTok can spread rapidly, often reaching millions of users in a matter of hours or days.

As we look toward the 2028 election, TikTok's influence will likely expand further. Political campaigns will increasingly use the platform to create snackable, viral content that resonates with younger voters. Candidates will need to adapt to this new style of communication, which values authenticity, creativity, and relatability. Unlike the polished and carefully curated posts on platforms like Instagram, TikTok's success is driven by organic and often unscripted videos that feel more personal.

Campaigns may also partner with influencers on TikTok to reach wider audiences. During the 2020 U.S. presidential election, TikTok influencers played a significant role in raising awareness about voting, voter registration, and political issues. As influencer marketing continues to grow, we can expect political campaigns to invest more in partnerships with influential TikTok creators to spread their messages.

—~—

Changing Regulations and Their Impact on Election Influence

As social media's role in elections has grown, so too has the need for regulation to ensure transparency, accountability, and fairness. In recent years, governments and social media companies have faced increased scrutiny over how platforms are used to influence elections, particularly in relation to misinformation, foreign interference, and data privacy.

Regulating Political Ads on Social Media

One of the key areas where regulations have evolved is the treatment of political ads on social media. In the wake of the 2016 U.S. election, it became evident that social media platforms were vulnerable to the spread of misinformation and manipulation, including foreign interference. In response, platforms like Facebook introduced more stringent policies regarding political advertising. For example, Facebook now requires political advertisers to disclose who paid for the ad and where the money came from, offering greater transparency to users.

As we approach 2028, we can expect these regulations to become even more robust. Governments are likely to impose stricter rules around how political ads are targeted, particularly when it comes to microtargeting—a strategy that allows campaigns to deliver personalized ads to specific voter segments based on their online behavior. While microtargeting has proven to be a powerful tool for campaigns, critics argue that it can also be used to manipulate voters by delivering tailored misinformation or exploiting voters' fears and biases.

Regulating "Deepfakes"

There may also be increased regulation around "deepfakes"—videos or images that use artificial intelligence to create realistic but fake portrayals of people saying or doing things they never actually did. Deepfakes have the potential to cause significant harm in elections by spreading disinformation about candidates. To combat this, governments may introduce deepfake detection technologies or penalties for those who create or share deepfake content with the intent to deceive voters.

The Power of Algorithms in Shaping Political Narratives

One of the most critical factors influencing elections in the future will be the power of algorithms. Social media algorithms are designed to prioritize content that generates high engagement, which often means that controversial or emotionally charged content rises to the top of users' feeds. While this helps drive user interaction, it also means that polarizing content—whether true or not—can dominate online political discourse.

In the 2028 election, the role of algorithms will be even more pronounced. Platforms like TikTok, Facebook, and Instagram will continue to use algorithms to determine which content users see, potentially shaping their perceptions of candidates and issues. This has raised concerns about the creation of echo chambers, where users are only exposed to content that aligns with their existing beliefs, reinforcing polarization and reducing the likelihood of meaningful dialogue between opposing viewpoints.

To address these concerns, social media companies may need to make their algorithms more transparent and provide users with greater control over what content they see. For example, platforms could offer users the option to view content chronologically rather than algorithmically, or provide tools to diversify the sources of information in their feeds.

--~--

The Role of Artificial Intelligence and Automation

As technology continues to advance, artificial intelligence (AI) and automation will play an increasingly important role in elections. AI-powered tools can help political campaigns analyze voter behavior, predict election outcomes, and optimize campaign strategies in real time. For example, AI can be used to create personalized campaign messages for millions of voters, allowing campaigns to target individuals with pinpoint accuracy.

However, AI and automation also present challenges, particularly when it comes to misinformation. AI-driven bots can flood social media platforms with false information or amplify divisive content, making it difficult for users to distinguish between real and fake accounts. As AI becomes more sophisticated, platforms and governments will need to develop tools to detect and counter these automated systems.

--~--

The Future of Political Engagement: Direct Voter-Candidate Interaction

One of the most exciting developments in the future of social media and elections is the potential for more direct engagement between voters and candidates. Platforms like Twitter have already made it possible for citizens to ask questions, voice concerns, and engage in real-time conversations with political leaders. Moving forward, we can expect even more opportunities for voters to interact directly with candidates.

Live streaming, town halls, and Q&A sessions on platforms like YouTube, Instagram, and TikTok will likely become more common, providing voters with opportunities to hear directly from candidates in an unscripted format. This form of direct interaction can foster greater trust and transparency, allowing candidates to connect with voters on a personal level.

Additionally, new technologies such as virtual reality (VR) and augmented reality (AR) could create more immersive ways for candidates to engage with voters. Imagine a future where voters can attend virtual rallies, meet candidates in virtual environments, or participate in virtual debates—all from the comfort of their homes.

As we look toward the 2028 election and beyond, social media will continue to shape how elections are fought and won. Evolving platforms like TikTok, changing regulations, and advances in artificial intelligence will all play a critical role in determining how political campaigns communicate with voters and how voters engage with the political process. While social media offers unprecedented opportunities for political engagement and outreach, it also presents challenges, particularly when it comes to misinformation, algorithmic manipulation, and data privacy.

As these platforms and technologies evolve, it is crucial for both governments and tech companies to work together to ensure that social media remains a force for good in democratic elections, promoting transparency, accountability, and informed civic participation. Ultimately, the future of social media in elections will depend on how we navigate these challenges and harness the power of technology to strengthen, rather than undermine, the democratic process.

Chapter 10

~~~~

Conclusion:

Your Role in the 2024 Election Power, Informed Choices, and Digital Participation
~~~~

As the 2024 election approaches, your role as a voter has never been more crucial. Whether you're casting a vote in a local, state, or national election, your decision will shape the policies and leaders that will influence the future of your country. In this digital age, the way you engage with information—particularly through social media—plays a significant part in making informed choices and exercising your digital voice. Understanding your power as a voter, navigating social media responsibly, and staying engaged online are essential steps to ensuring that your vote contributes to a better future.

Understanding Your Power as a Voter

One of the most important roles you play in any election is that of a voter. Regardless of the size or scale of the election, your vote matters. History has shown that elections can be won or lost by slim margins, particularly in swing states or local races. Each vote contributes to the overall democratic process, ensuring that elected officials reflect the will of the people.

However, being an informed voter requires more than just showing up at the polls. It's essential to take the time to understand the candidates and their policies. As a voter, your power lies in your ability to hold leaders accountable, evaluate their platforms, and make choices that reflect the kind of future you want for your community and country.

For example, if climate change is important to you, carefully examine how each candidate plans to address environmental issues and consider their past record on the topic. If healthcare is your priority, look at how different candidates propose to reform the system. By being well-informed, you ensure that your vote is a reflection of your values and long-term priorities.

Navigating Social Media to Make Informed Choices

In the era of social media, political campaigns are increasingly fought online, and platforms like Facebook, Twitter, TikTok, and Instagram are key battlegrounds for influencing voter behavior. While social media provides easy access to political information, it also poses challenges, particularly when it comes to misinformation and echo chambers.

To make informed choices, it's important to navigate social media critically. Here are some key tips for doing so:

Diversify Your Sources: Follow a wide range of media outlets, including those with different political perspectives. This helps ensure that you're exposed to a variety of viewpoints and reduces the likelihood of being trapped in an echo chamber.

Fact-Check Information: Social media is notorious for the spread of false or misleading information. Before believing or sharing a sensational post, take a moment to verify its accuracy. Websites like FactCheck.org, Snopes, and Politifact are valuable tools for confirming the truthfulness of a claim.

Be Skeptical of Viral Content: Just because something has gone viral doesn't mean it's accurate. Viral posts often appeal to emotions, such as fear or outrage, rather than fact. Approach viral political content with a healthy dose of skepticism and cross-reference it with reliable sources.

By being mindful of these tips, you can avoid falling into the trap of misinformation and ensure that the political decisions you make are based on credible and well-researched information.

--~--

Using Your Digital Voice: Participating and Staying Informed on Social Media

Beyond casting your vote, social media gives you the opportunity to participate in the democratic process in real-time. Platforms like Twitter allow you to engage directly with candidates, ask questions, and express your views. This level of interaction bridges the gap between citizens and their representatives, allowing for greater transparency and accountability.

Engaging in discussions on social media can also help raise awareness about important issues. By sharing credible information, participating in political conversations, and advocating for the causes you believe in, you contribute to the public discourse. Your digital voice matters, and by using it, you can help shape political narratives and inspire others to get involved.

However, it's important to participate responsibly. Avoid inflammatory or divisive rhetoric, and seek out meaningful conversations with people who may hold different views. Productive dialogue is essential to a healthy democracy, and social media can be a powerful tool for fostering understanding and collaboration across political divides.

--~--

Your Role in Shaping the Future

The 2024 election is a pivotal moment in history, and your role as a voter extends far beyond simply casting a ballot. By making informed choices, critically navigating social media, and using your digital voice to participate in the political process, you can contribute to a more informed and engaged electorate. The decisions made in this election will shape the future for generations to come, and your vote—and your voice—are powerful tools for ensuring that future reflects your values and priorities.

In the end, democracy thrives on informed, active participation. Whether through voting, sharing information online, or engaging in meaningful political conversations, you have the power to make a difference in the 2024 election and beyond.

61

Appendices

<u>Register to Vote</u>

Alabama	https://www.sos.alabama.gov/alabama-votes/voter/register-to-vote
Alaska	https://www.elections.alaska.gov/voter-information/#Reg
Arizona	https://azsos.gov/elections/voters/registering-vote
Arkansas	https://www.sos.arkansas.gov/elections/voter-information/voter-registration-information
California	https://registertovote.ca.gov/
Colorado	https://www.sos.state.co.us/voter/pages/pub/olvr/verifyNewVoter.xhtml
Connecticut	https://portal.ct.gov/sots/election-services/voter-information/voter-registration-information
Delaware	https://elections.delaware.gov/voter/votereg.shtml
District of Columbia	https://www.dcboe.org/voters/register-to-vote/register-update-voter-registration
Florida	https://registertovoteflorida.gov/home
Georgia	https://mvp.sos.ga.gov/s/
Hawaii	https://olvr.hawaii.gov/
Idaho	https://elections.sos.idaho.gov/ElectionLink/ElectionLink/ApplicationInstructions.aspx
Illinois	https://ova.elections.il.gov/
Indiana	https://indianavoters.in.gov/
Iowa	https://sos.iowa.gov/elections/voterinformation/voterregistration.html
Kansas	https://www.kdor.ks.gov/apps/voterreg/home/index
Kentucky	https://vrsws.sos.ky.gov/ovrweb/
Louisiana	https://www.sos.la.gov/ElectionsAndVoting/RegisterToVote/Pages/default.aspx
Maine	https://www.maine.gov/sos/cec/elec/voter-info/votreg.html
Maryland	https://www.elections.maryland.gov/voter_registration/index.html
Massachusetts	https://www.sec.state.ma.us/divisions/elections/voter-resources/registering-to-vote.htm
Michigan	https://www.michigan.gov/sos/elections/voting/register-to-vote
Minnesota	https://www.sos.state.mn.us/elections-voting/register-to-vote/
Mississippi	https://www.sos.ms.gov/voter-id/register
Missouri	https://www.sos.mo.gov/elections/goVoteMissouri/register
Montana	https://sosmt.gov/elections/voter-file/
Nebraska	https://sos.nebraska.gov/elections/registering-vote
Nevada	https://www.nvsos.gov/sos/elections/voters/registering-to-vote
New Hampshire	https://www.sos.nh.gov/elections/register-vote
New Jersey	https://nj.gov/state/elections/voter-registration.shtml
New Mexico	https://www.sos.nm.gov/voting-and-elections/voter-information-portal-nmvote-org/voter-registration-information/
New York	https://dmv.ny.gov/more-info/electronic-voter-registration-application
North Carolina	https://www.ncsbe.gov/registering/how-register
North Dakota	https://www.sos.nd.gov/elections/voter
Ohio	https://olvr.ohiosos.gov/
Oklahoma	https://oklahoma.gov/elections/voter-registration/register-to-vote.html
Oregon	https://sos.oregon.gov/voting/Pages/registration.aspx
Pennsylvania	https://www.pa.gov/en/agencies/vote/voter-registration.html
Rhode Island	https://vote.sos.ri.gov/Home/RegistertoVote?ActiveFlag=1
South Carolina	https://scvotes.gov/voters/register-to-vote/
South Dakota	https://sdsos.gov/elections-voting/voting/register-to-vote/default.aspx
Tennessee	https://sos.tn.gov/elections/guides/how-to-register-to-vote
Texas	https://www.votetexas.gov/register-to-vote/index.html
Utah	https://secure.utah.gov/voterreg/index.html
Vermont	https://sos.vermont.gov/elections/voters/registration/

Virginia	https://vote.elections.virginia.gov/VoterInformation/Lookup/status
Washington	https://www.sos.wa.gov/elections/voters/voter-eligibility-resources/voter-eligibility
West Virginia	https://ovr.sos.wv.gov/Register/Landing
Wisconsin	https://myvote.wi.gov/en-us/Register-To-Vote
Wyoming	https://sos.wyo.gov/Elections/State/RegisteringToVote.aspx

Fact-Checking Websites

1. <u>FactCheck.org</u> - https://www.factcheck.org/
   - ➢ A nonpartisan website run by the Annenberg Public Policy Center. It monitors the factual accuracy of statements made by U.S. politicians in TV ads, debates, speeches, and interviews.

2. <u>PolitiFact</u> - https://www.politifact.com/
   - ➢ Run by the Poynter Institute, PolitiFact fact-checks political claims and rates them on a scale from "True" to "Pants on Fire." They focus heavily on statements from U.S. political figures and campaign content.

3. <u>Snopes</u> - https://www.snopes.com/
   - ➢ A well-known website that debunks misinformation, rumors, and urban legends. During election cycles, they focus on false claims, rumors, and viral stories about candidates.

4. <u>The Washington Post Fact Checker</u>
   https://www.washingtonpost.com/politics/fact-checker/
   - ➢ The Washington Post's Fact Checker scrutinizes statements from U.S. politicians and campaigns, awarding "Pinocchios" based on the level of falsehood.

5. <u>Reuters Fact Check</u> - https://www.reuters.com/fact-check/
   - ➢ Reuters provides fact-checks on misleading claims, especially those that spread across social media during election cycles.

6. <u>Associated Press Fact Check</u> - https://apnews.com/ap-fact-check
   - ➢ AP News offers a reliable fact-checking service that targets misinformation and misinterpretations of U.S. politics and electoral claims.

7. <u>Lead Stories</u> - https://www.leadstories.com/
   - ➢ A lesser-known fact-checking service that is part of Facebook's efforts to combat fake news. It covers viral stories, particularly those spreading on social media.

8. <u>OpenSecrets.org</u> - https://www.opensecrets.org/
   - ➢ Although not exclusively a fact-checking website, OpenSecrets tracks campaign finance and lobbying, providing important context about where candidates' support comes from, which can help voters fact-check claims about political donations.

9. <u>BBC Reality Check</u> - https://www.bbc.com/news/reality_check
   - ➢ The BBC offers fact-checking for international and U.S.-based political events, focusing on debunking misinformation surrounding elections.

10. <u>TruthOrFiction.com</u> - https://www.truthorfiction.com/
    - ➢ A site that investigates the accuracy of rumors, viral posts, and misleading claims, often focused on U.S. politics and elections.

These websites provide a wide range of resources for verifying the accuracy of political statements, viral content, and claims made by politicians in the 2024 election.

2024 Presidential Candidates

Here are links to the platforms of the key candidates for the 2024 U.S. presidential election:

1. **Donald Trump** – The former president's platform focuses on America First policies, economic growth, immigration reform, and foreign policy shifts. You can explore his platform on his campaign website:

    ➢ Donald Trump Campaign Website - https://www.donaldjtrump.com/

2. **Kamala Harris** – As Vice President, Harris has focused on expanding healthcare access, environmental justice, economic recovery, and civil rights. You can find more about her policy plans on her campaign website

    ➢ Kamala Harris Campaign Website - https://kamalaharris.com/

3. **Cornel West** – Running under the Green Party, West advocates for racial justice, economic equality, and progressive reforms. His platform can be found on his campaign website:

    ➢ Cornel West Campaign Website - https://www.cornelwest2024.com/

4. **Chase Oliver** – Representing the Libertarian Party, Oliver promotes personal freedom, small government, and free-market principles. More about his platform can be found here:

    ➢ Chase Oliver Campaign Website - https://votechaseoliver.com/

Each of these links will provide you with more in-depth information about their policies and campaign promises.